Impressum
Verlag: BABADADA GmbH, Nedderfeld 112 , 22529 Hamburg
Geschäftsführer / Verlagsleitung: Harald Hof
Druck: Books on Demand GmbH, In de Tarpen 42, 22848 Norderstedt

Imprint
Publisher: BABADADA GmbH, Nedderfeld 112 , 22529 Hamburg, Germany
Managing Director / Publishing direction: Harald Hof
Print: Books on Demand GmbH, In de Tarpen 42, 22848 Norderstedt

school
skóli

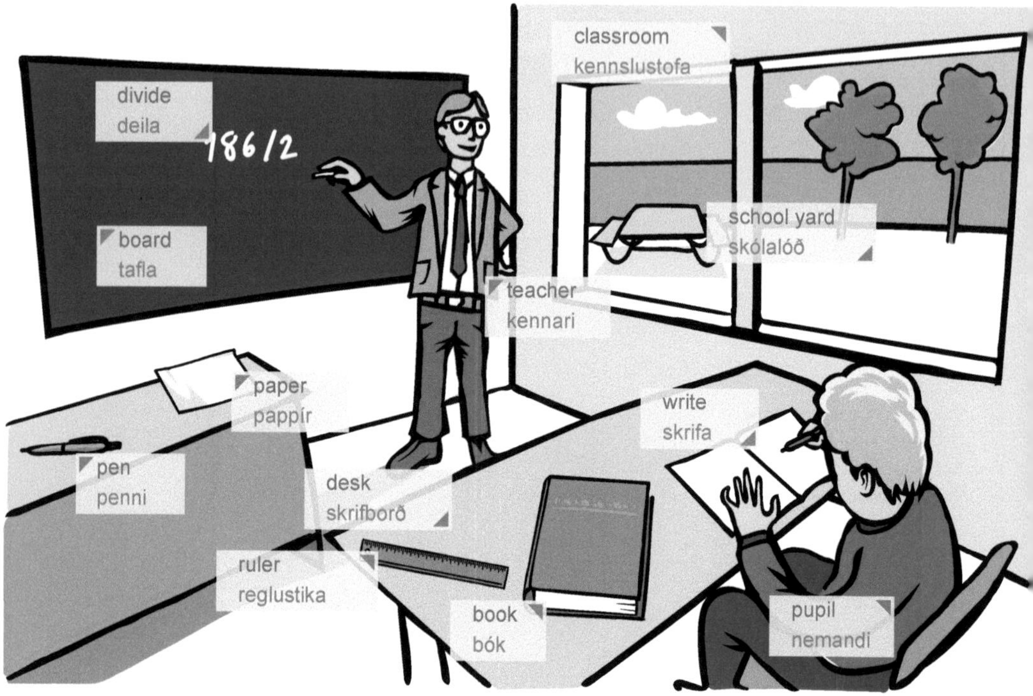
classroom
kennslustofa
divide
deila
186/2
board
tafla
school yard
skólalóð
teacher
kennari
paper
pappír
write
skrifa
pen
penni
desk
skrifborð
ruler
reglustika
book
bók
pupil
nemandi

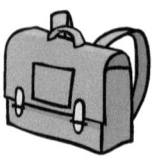

satchel
skólataska

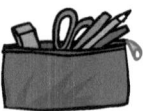

pencil case
pennaveski

pencil
blýantur

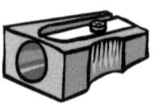

pencil sharpener
yddari

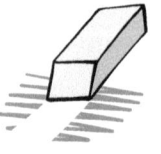

rubber
strokleður

drawing pad
teikniblað

drawing
teikning

paintbrush
pensill

paint box
litakassi

scissors
skæri

glue
lím

exercise book
æfingabók

homework
heimavinna

number
númer

add
leggja saman

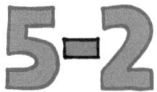

subtract
draga frá

multiply
margfalda

calculate
reikna

letter
bréf

alphabet
stafróf

word
orð

text

texti

read

lesa

chalk

krít

lesson

kennslustund

register

kladdi

exam

próf

certificate

vottorð

school uniform

skólabúningur

education

menntun

encyclopedia

alfræðirit

university

háskóli

microscope

smásjá

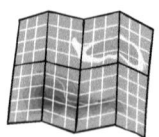

map

kort

waste-paper basket

ruslakarfa

travel
ferðalög

hotel
hótel
Grand
hostel
farfuglaheimili
ROOMS
bureau de change
gjaldeyrisskipti
CHANGE
car
bíll

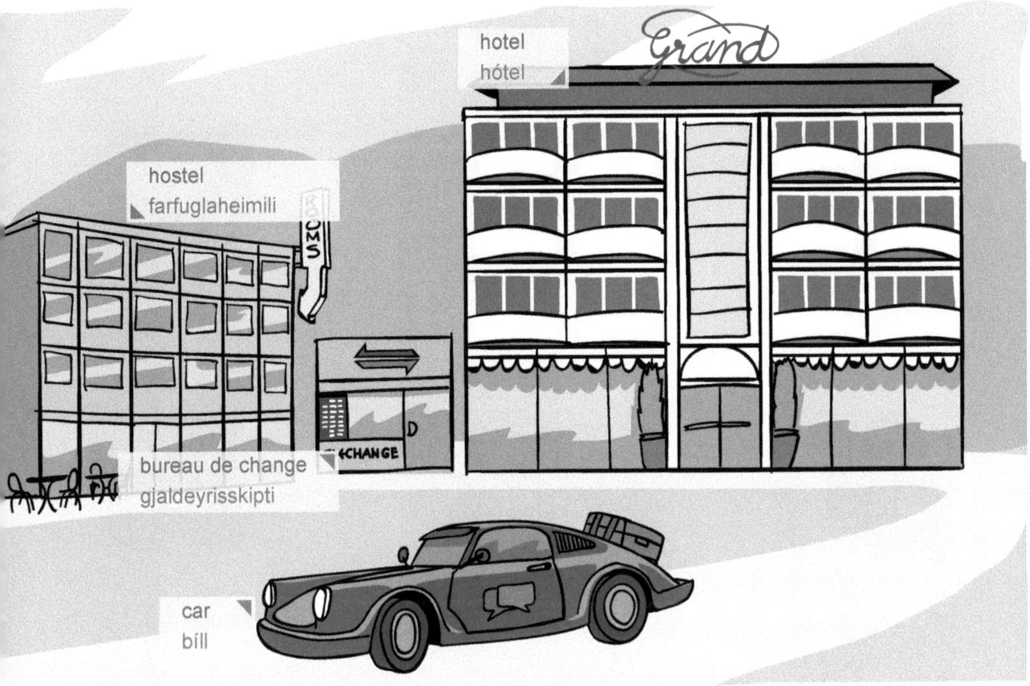

language
tungumál

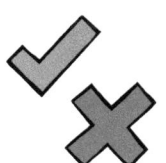

yes / no
já / nei

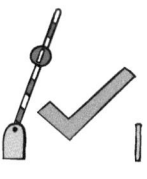

Okay
allt í lagi

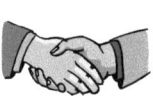

hello
halló

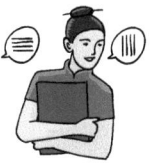

translator
þýðandi

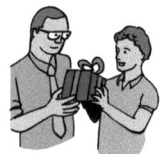

Thank you
takk fyrir

how much is...?

hvað kostar...?

I do not understand

Ég skil ekki

problem

vandamál

Good evening!

Gott kvöld!

Good morning!

Góðan dag!

Good night!

Góða nótt!

bye bye

bless bless

direction

átt

luggage

farangur

bag

taska

backpack

bakpoki

guest

gestur

room

herbergi

sleeping bag

svefnpoki

tent

tjald

tourist information

upplýsingamiðstöð

beach

strönd

credit card

kreditkort

breakfast

morgunverður

lunch

hádegisverður

dinner

kvöldmatur

ticket

farmiði

lift

lyfta

stamp

frímerki

border

landamæri

customs

tollur

embassy

sendiráð

visa

vegabréfsáritun

passport

vegabréf

travel - ferðalög

transport
samgöngur

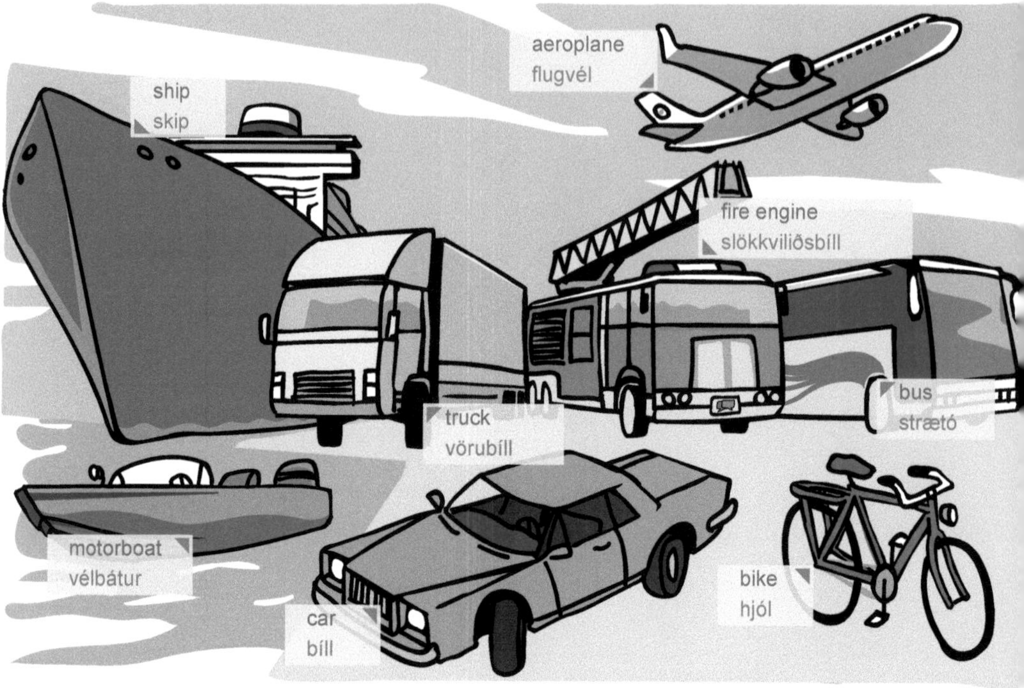
aeroplane
flugvél
ship
skip
fire engine
slökkviliðsbíll
bus
strætó
truck
vörubíll
motorboat
vélbátur
bike
hjól
car
bíll

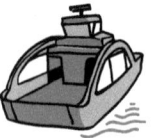

ferry
ferja

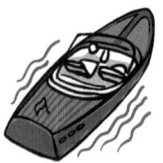

boat
bátur

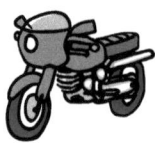

motorbike
mótorhjól

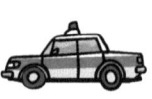

police car
lögreglubíll

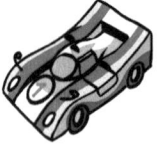

racing car
kappakstursbíll

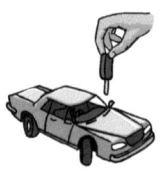

rental car
bílaleigubíll

car sharing

bílasamneyti

breakdown truck

dráttarbíll

refuse truck

öskubíll

motor

vél

fuel

eldsneyti

petrol station

bensínstöð

traffic sign

umferðarskilti

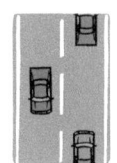

traffic

umferð

traffic jam

umferðarteppa

car park

bílastæði

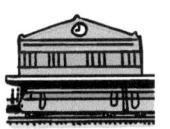

train station

lestarstöð

tracks

járnbrautarteinar

train

lest

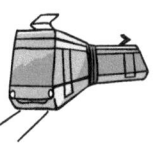

tram

sporvagn

carriage

vagn

helicopter

þyrla

airport

flugvöllur

tower

turn

passenger

farþegi

container

gámur

carton

pappakassi

cart

kerra

basket

karfa

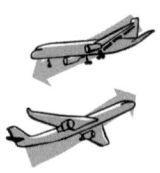

take off / land

takast á loft / lenda

city

borg

village

þorp

city centre

miðbær

house

hús

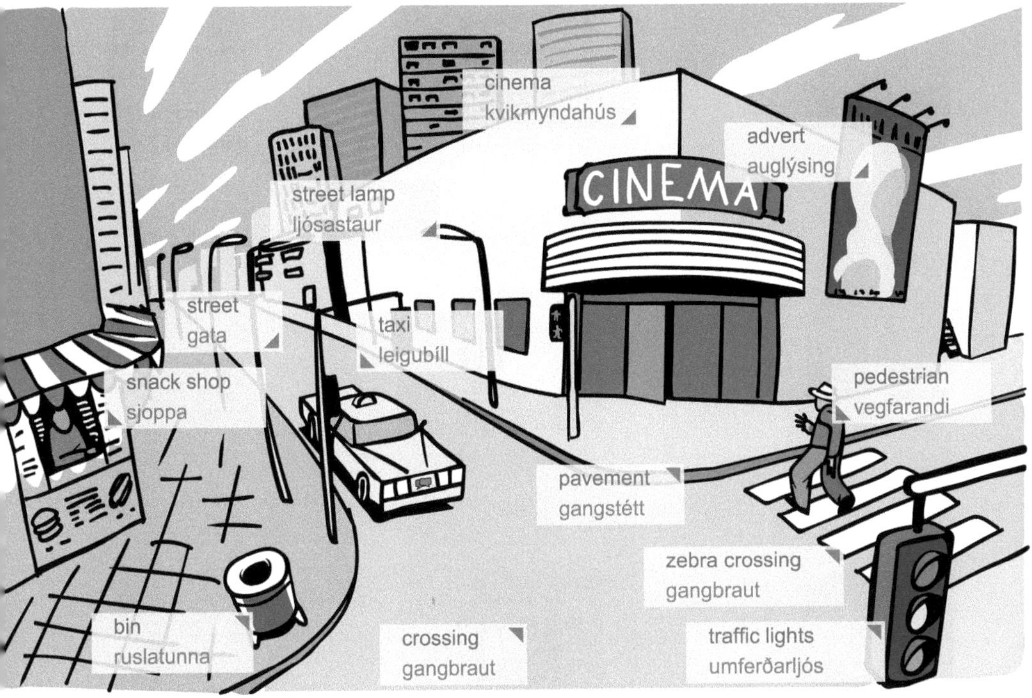
cinema
kvikmyndahús
CINEMA
advert
auglýsing
street lamp
ljósastaur
street
gata
taxi
leigubíll
snack shop
sjoppa
pedestrian
vegfarandi
pavement
gangstétt
zebra crossing
gangbraut
bin
ruslatunna
crossing
gangbraut
traffic lights
umferðarljós

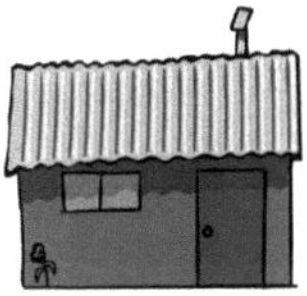
hut
skáli

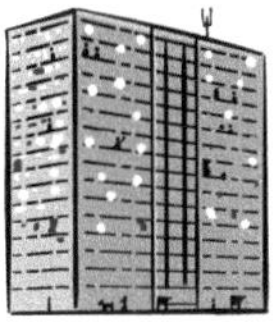
flat
íbúð

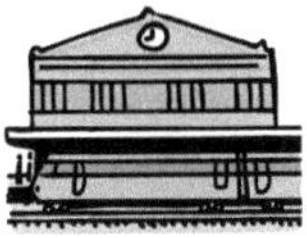
train station
lestarstöð

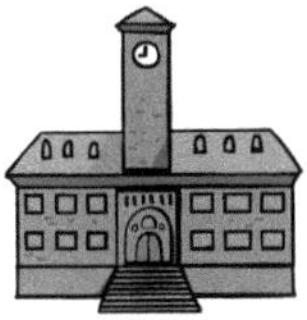
town hall
ráðhús

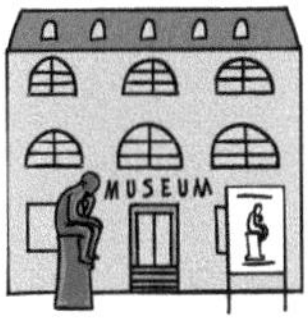
MUSEUM
museum
safn

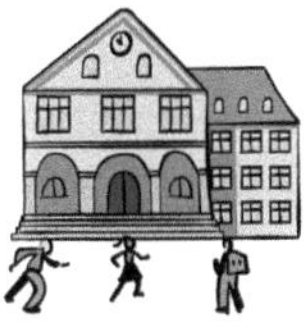
school
skóli

university

háskóli

bank

banki

hospital

sjúkrahús

hotel

hótel

pharmacy

apótek

office

skrifstofa

book shop

bókabúð

shop

búð

florist's

blómabúð

supermarket

kjörbúð

market

markaður

department store

stórmarkaður

fishmonger's

fiskbúð

shopping centre

verslunarmiðstöð

harbour

höfn

park

almenningsgarður

bench

bekkur

bridge

brú

stairs

stigi

underground

neðanjarðarlest

tunnel

göng

bus stop

biðstöð

bar

bar

restaurant

veitingastaður

postbox

póstkassi

street sign

götuskilti

parking meter

stöðumælir

zoo

dýragarður

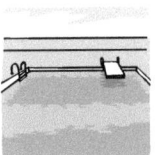

swimming pool

sundlaug

mosque

moska

farm

bær

pollution

mengun

graveyard

kirkjugarður

church

kirkja

playground

leiksvæði

temple

musteri

landscape
landslag

signpost
leiðarvísir

way
leið

meadow
engi

stone
steinn

hiker
göngufólk

tree
tré

river
á

grass
gras

flower
blóm

valley

dalur

hill

hæð

lake

stöðuvatn

forest

skógur

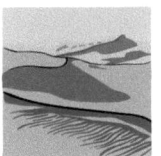

desert

eyðimörk

volcano

eldfjall

castle

kastali

rainbow

regnbogi

mushroom

sveppur

palm tree

pálmatré

mosquito

moskítófluga

fly

fluga

ant

maur

bee

býfluga

spider

kónguló

beetle

bjalla

frog

froskur

squirrel

íkorni

hedgehog

broddgöltur

hare

héri

owl

ugla

bird

fugl

swan

svanur

boar

villisvín

deer

dádýr

moose

elgur

dam

stífla

wind turbine

vindmylla

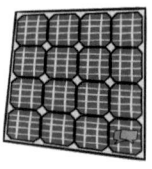

solar panel

sólarrafhlaða

climate

loftslag

restaurant
veitingastaður

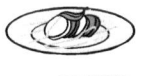

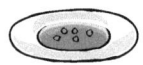

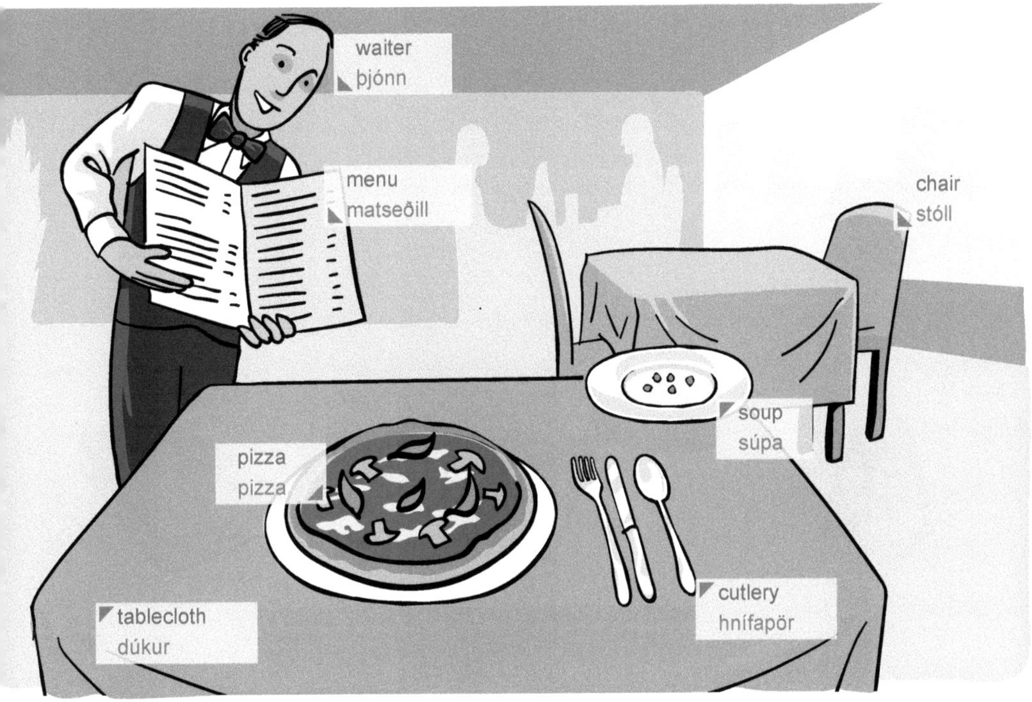

waiter
þjónn
menu
matseðill
chair
stóll
soup
súpa
pizza
pizza
cutlery
hnífapör
tablecloth
dúkur

starter
....
forréttur

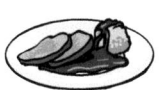

main course
....
aðalréttur

dessert
....
eftirréttur

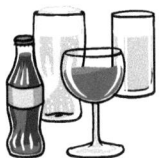

drinks
....
drykkir

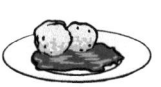

food
....
matur

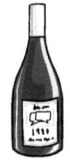

bottle
....
flaska

fast food

skyndibiti

street food

götumatur

teapot

teketill

sugar bowl

sykurskál

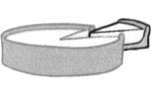

portion

skammtur

espresso machine

espressovél

high chair

barnastóll

bill

reikningur

tray

bakki

knife

hnífur

fork

gaffall

spoon

skeið

teaspoon

teskeið

serviette

servíetta

glass

glas

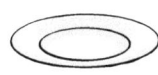

plate

diskur

soup plate

súpudiskur

saucer

undirskál

sauce

sósa

salt pot

saltstaukur

pepper mill

piparkvörn

vinegar

edik

oil

olía

spices

krydd

ketchup

tómatsósa

mustard

sinnep

mayonnaise

majónes

supermarket
kjörbúð

special offer
tilboð
FOR
customer
viðskiptavinur
dairy
mjólkurvörur
fruit
ávöxtur
trolley
búðarkerra

BUTCHERS

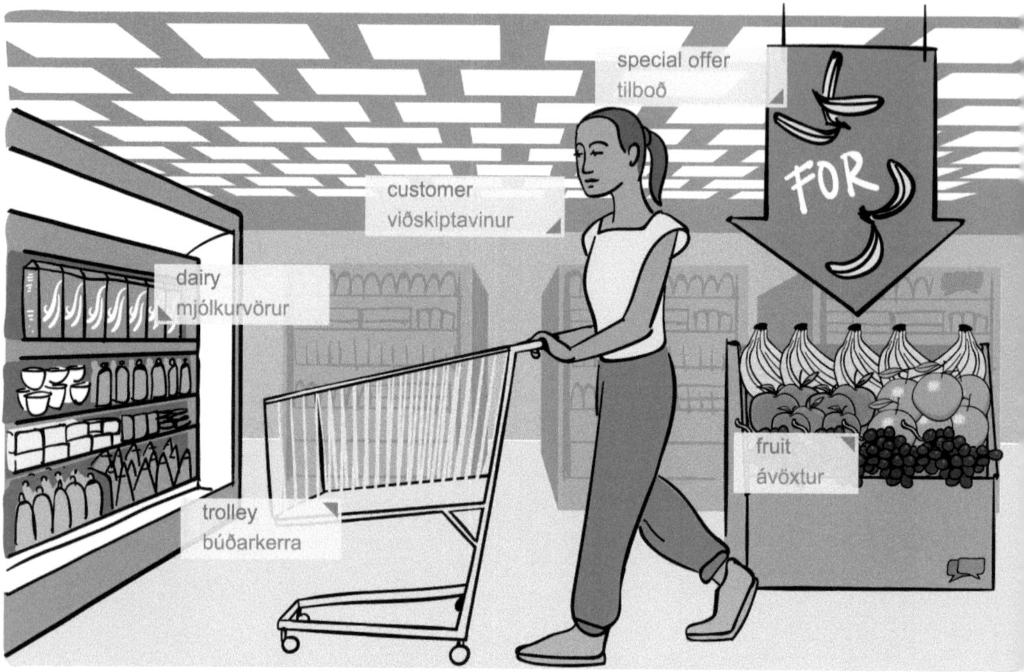

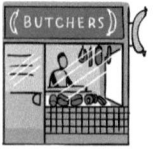

butcher´s

slátrari

BAKERY

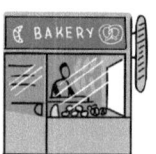

baker´s

bakarí

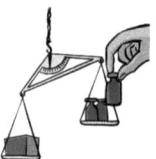

weigh

vega

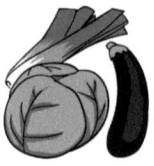

vegetables

grænmeti

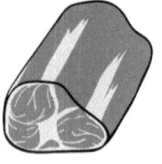

meat

kjöt

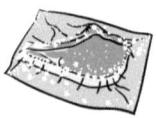

frozen food

frosinn matur

cold meat
kjötálegg

tinned food
niðursoðinn matur

washing powder
þvottaefni

sweets
sælgæti

household products
vörur til heimilisnota

cleaning products
hreinsiefni

salesperson
afgreiðslukona

till
afgreiðslukassi

cashier
gjaldkeri

shopping list
innkaupalisti

opening hours
opnunartímar

wallet
veski

credit card
kreditkort

bag
poki

plastic bag
plastpoki

water

vatn

juice

safi

milk

mjólk

coke

kók

wine

vín

beer

bjór

alcohol

áfengi

cocoa

kakó

tea

te

coffee

kaffi

espresso

espresso

cappuccino

kaffi

banana

banani

apple

epli

orange

appelsínugulur

melon

melóna

lemon

sítróna

carrot

gulrót

garlic

hvítlaukur

bamboo

bambus

onion

laukur

mushroom

sveppir

nuts

hnetur

noodles

núðlur

spaghetti

spagettí

rice

hrísgrjón

salad

salat

chips

franskar kartöflur

fried potatoes

steiktar kartöflur

pizza

pizza

hamburger

hamborgari

sandwich

samloka

cutlet

snitsel

ham

skinka

salami

salami

sausage

pylsa

chicken

kjúklingur

roast

steik

fish

fiskur

porridge oats

haframjöl

muesli

múslí

cornflakes

kornflögur

flour

hveiti

croissant

franskt horn

bread roll

smábrauð

bread

brauð

toast

ristað brauð

biscuits

kex

butter

smjör

curd

ystingur

cake

kaka

egg

egg

fried egg

spælt egg

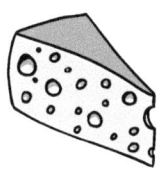

cheese

ostur

ice cream

ís

sugar

sykur

honey

hunang

jam

sulta

chocolate spread

súkkulaðiálegg

curry

karrý

farm
bær

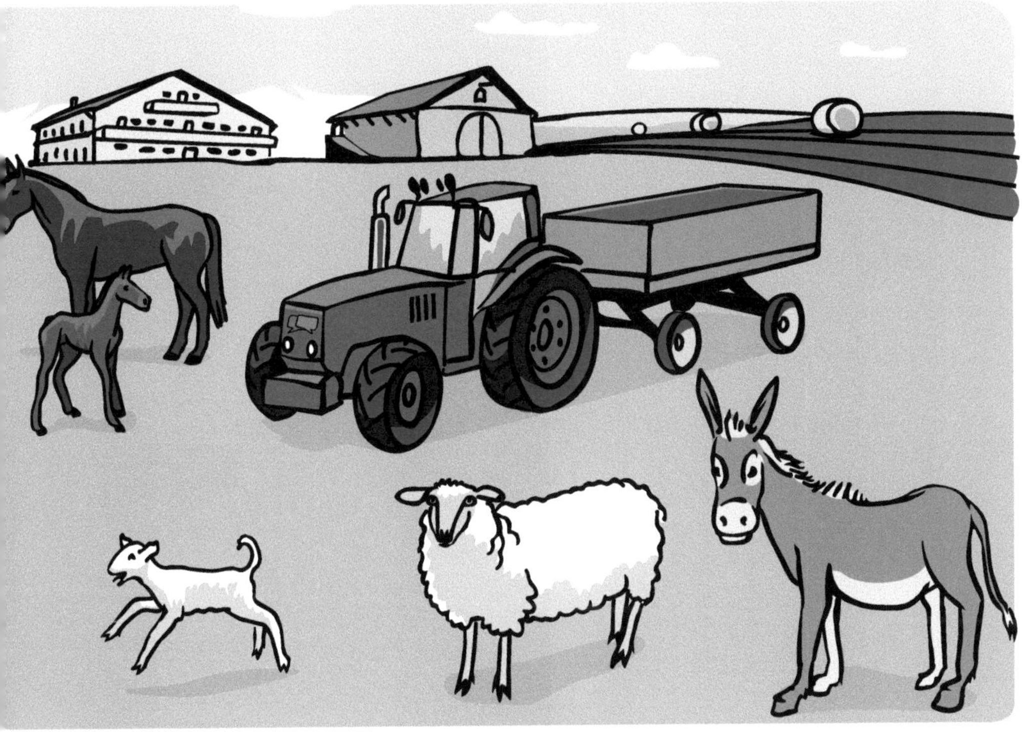

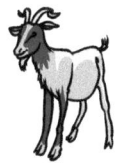

goat
geit

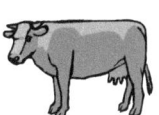

cow
kýr

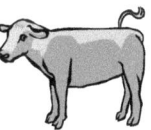

calf
kálfur

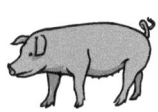

pig
svín

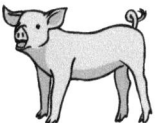

piglet
grís

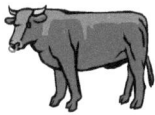

bull
naut

goose

gæs

duck

önd

chick

ungi

hen

hæna

cock

hani

rat

rotta

cat

köttur

mouse

mús

ox

uxi

dog

hundur

doghouse

hundakofi

garden hose

garðslanga

watering can

garðkanna

scythe

ljár

plough

plógur

sickle

sigð

hoe

hlújárn

pitchfork

heygaffall

axe

öxi

wheelbarrow

hjólbörur

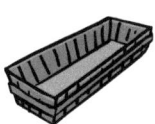

trough

trog

milk can

mjólkurfata

sack

poki

fence

girðing

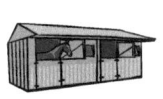

stable

gripahús

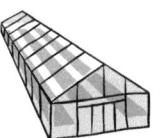

greenhouse

gróðurhús

soil

jarðvegur

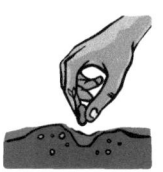

seed

fræ

fertilizer

áburður

combine harvester

kornskurðarvél

farm - bær

harvest

uppskera

harvest

uppskera

yams

kínverskar kartöflur

wheat

hveiti

soy

soja

potato

kartafla

corn

maís

rapeseed

repja

fruit tree

ávaxtatré

cassava

maníókarót

cereals

korn

house
hús

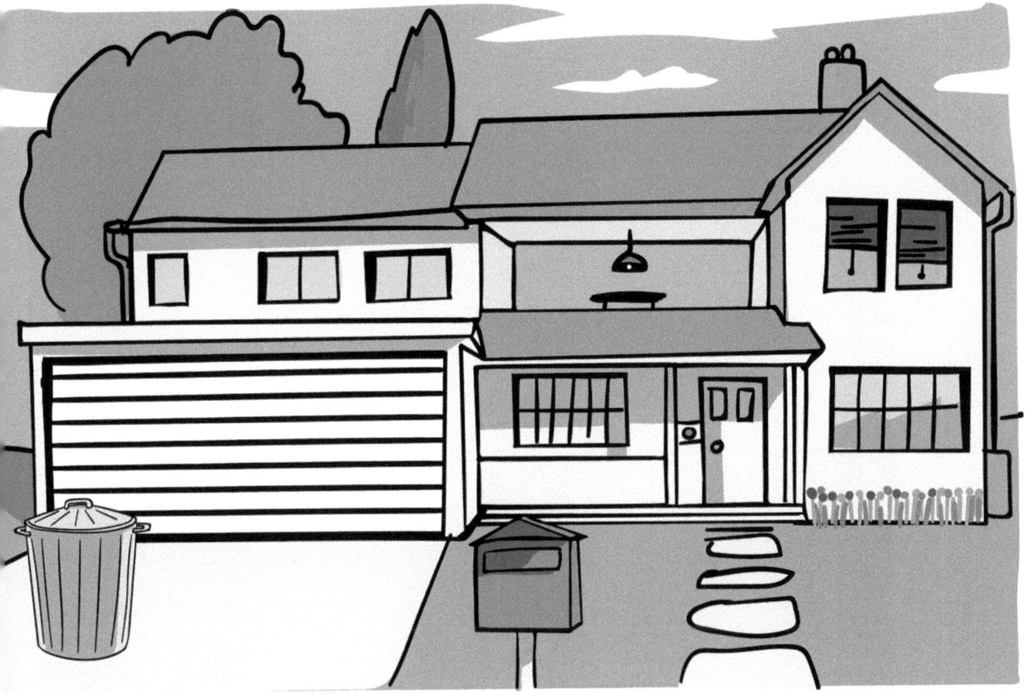

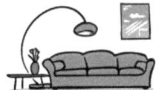

living room
....
stofa

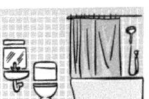

bathroom
....
baðherbergi

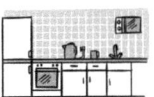

kitchen
....
eldhús

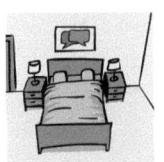

bedroom
....
svefnherbergi

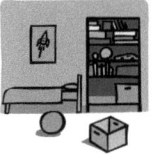

child's room
....
barnaherbergi

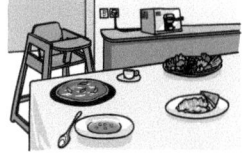

dining room
....
borðstofa

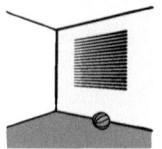

floor

gólf

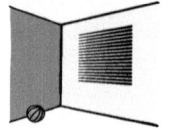

wall

veggur

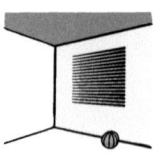

ceiling

loft

cellar

kjallari

sauna

gufubað

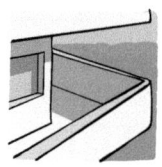

balcony

svalir

terrace

verönd

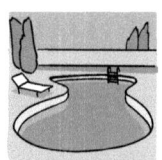

pool

sundlaug

lawn mower

sláttuvél

sheet

lak

bedspread

rúmteppi

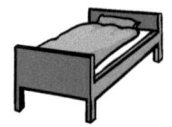

bed

rúm

broom

kústur

bucket

fata

switch

rofi

living room
stofa

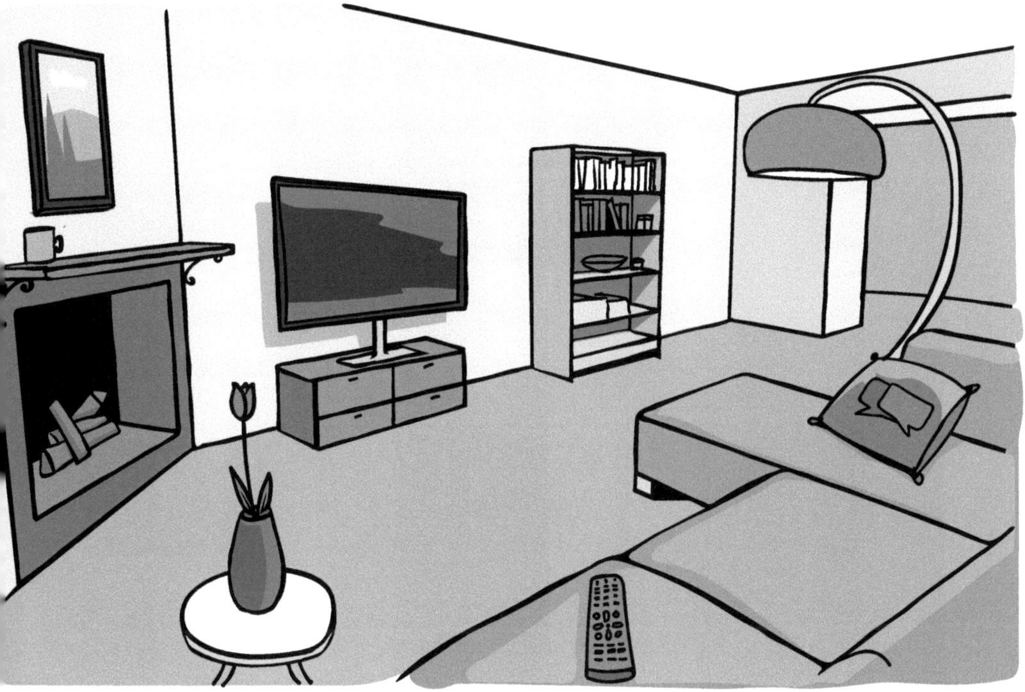

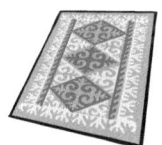

carpet

teppi

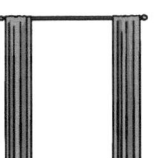

curtain

gardínur

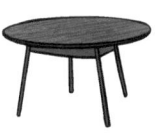

table

borð

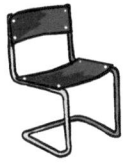

chair

stóll

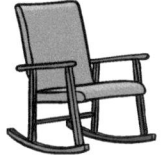

rocking chair

ruggustóll

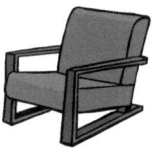

armchair

hægindastóll

book

bók

blanket

sæng

decoration

skraut

firewood

eldiviður

film

mynd

hi-fi equipment

hljómflutningstæki

key

lykill

newspaper

dagblað

painting

málverk

poster

veggspjald

radio

útvarp

notepad

minnisbók

hoover

ryksuga

cactus

kaktus

candle

kerti

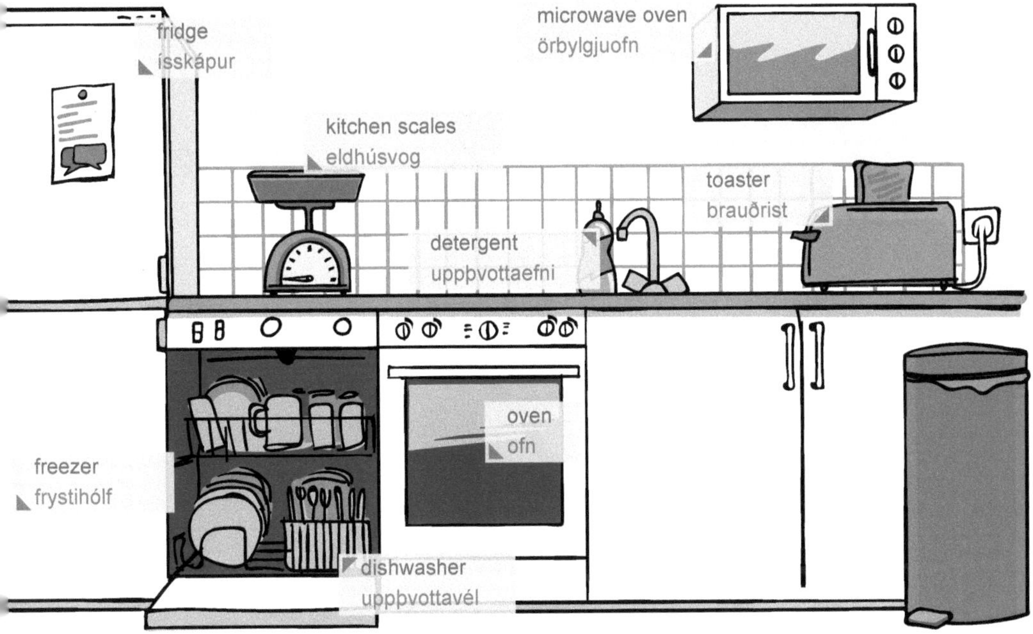

microwave oven
örbylgjuofn

fridge
isskápur

kitchen scales
eldhúsvog

toaster
brauðrist

detergent
uppþvottaefni

oven
ofn

freezer
frystihólf

dishwasher
uppþvottavél

cooker

eldavél

pot

pottur

cast-iron pot

steypujárnspottur

wok / kadai

wok/kadai

pan

panna

kettle

ketill

steamer

gufukarfa

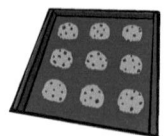

baking tray

ofnform

crockery

leirtau

mug

mál

bowl

skál

chopsticks

prjónar

ladle

ausa

spatula

spaði

whisk

pískur

strainer

sigti

sieve

málmsigti

grater

rifjárn

mortar

mortél

barbecue

grill

open fire

opinn eldur

chopping board

skurðarbretti

rolling pin

kökukefli

corkscrew

tappatogari

can

dós

can opener

dósaopnari

pot holder

pottaleppur

sink

vaskur

brush

bursti

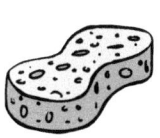

sponge

svampur

blender

blandari

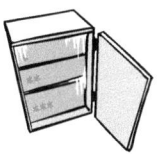

deep freezer

frystir

baby bottle

peli

tap

blöndunartæki

bathroom
baðherbergi

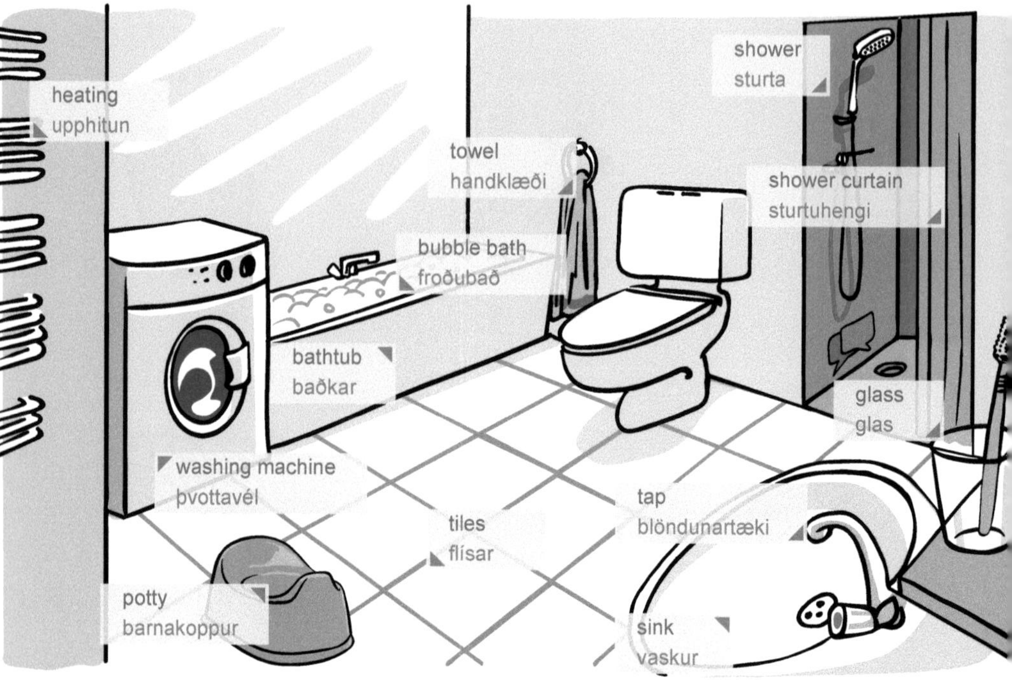

heating
upphitun

shower
sturta

towel
handklæði

shower curtain
sturtuhengi

bubble bath
froðubað

bathtub
baðkar

glass
glas

washing machine
þvottavél

tap
blöndunartæki

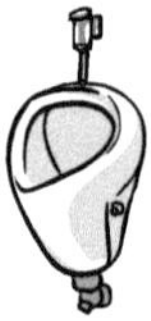

tiles
flísar

potty
barnakoppur

sink
vaskur

toilet	squat toilet	bidet
salerni	salerni án setu	skolskál

urinal	toilet paper	toilet brush
þvagskál	salernispappír	salernisbursti

toothbrush

tannbursti

toothpaste

tannkrem

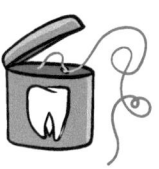

dental floss

tannþráður

wash

þvo

handheld shower

handsturta

douche

salernissturta

basin

vaskur

back brush

bakbursti

soap

sápa

shower gel

sturtugel

shampoo

sjampó

flannel

flannel

drain

niðurfall

cream

krem

deodorant

svitalyktareyðir

mirror
spegill

hand mirror
handspegill

razor
rakskafa

shaving foam
raksápa

aftershave
rakspíri

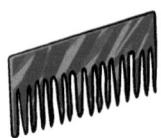

comb
greiða

brush
bursti

hair dryer
hárþurrka

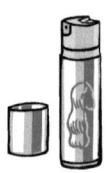

hairspray
hársprey

makeup
farði

lipstick
varalitur

nail varnish
naglalakk

cotton wool
bómull

nail scissors
naglaklippur

perfume
ilmvatn

washbag

þvottapoki

stool

kollur

weighing scale

vog

bathrobe

sloppur

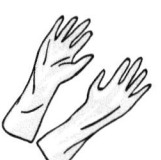

rubber gloves

gúmmíhanskar

tampon

tíðatappi

sanitary towel

dömubindi

chemical toilet

efnasalerni

child's room
barnaherbergi

alarm clock
vekjaraklukka
cuddly toy
mjúkt leikfang
toy car
leikfangabíll
rattle
hrista
doll's house
dúkkuhús
present
gjöf

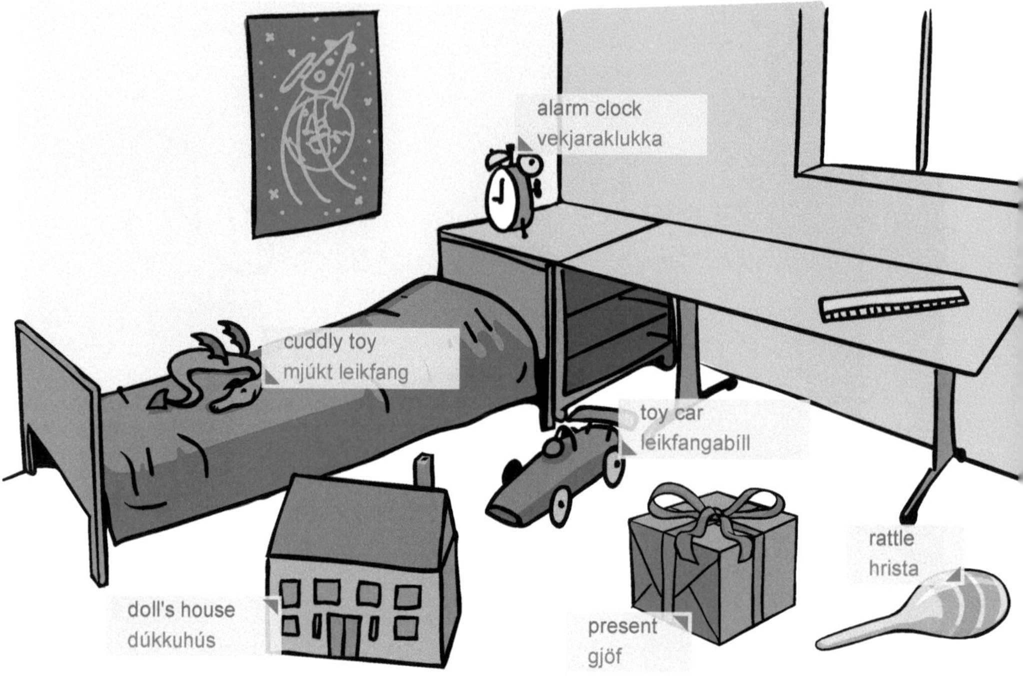

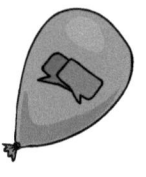

balloon

blaðra

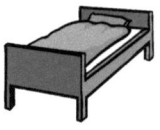

bed

rúm

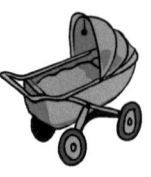

pram

barnavagn

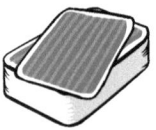

deck of cards

spilastokkur

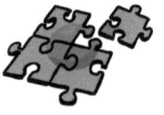

jigsaw

púsluspil

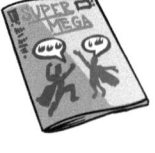

comic

myndasaga

lego bricks

legókubbar

building blocks

leikfangakubbar

action figure

leikfangakall

babygrow

samfestingur

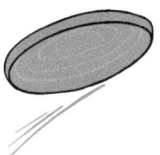

frisbee

Frisbídiskur

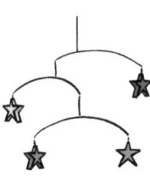

mobile

órói

board game

spilaborð

dice

teningar

model train set

lestarlíkan

dummy

snuð

party

veisla

picture book

myndabók

ball

bolti

doll

brúða

play

spila

sandpit

sandkassi

swing

sveifla

toys

leikföng

video game console

leikjatölva

tricycle

þríhjól

teddy bear

bangsi

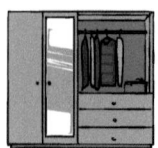

wardrobe

fataskápur

clothing

föt

socks

sokkar

stockings

kvensokkabuxur

tights

sokkabuxur

scarf
trefill

umbrella
regnhlíf

t-shirt
stuttermabolur

belt
belti

boots
skór

slippers
inniskór

trainers
strigaskór

sandals
sandalar

shoes
skór

rubber boots
gúmmístígvél

underpants
nærbuxur

bra
brjóstahaldari

vest
vesti

clothing - föt

45

body
samfella

trousers
buxur

jeans
gallabuxur

skirt
pils

blouse
blússa

shirt
skyrta

pullover
peysa

hoodie
hettupeysa

blazer
jakki

jacket
jakki

coat
frakki

raincoat
regnfrakki

costume
dragt

dress
kjóll

wedding dress
brúðarkjóll

suit

jakkaföt

nightgown

náttkjóll

pyjamas

náttföt

sari

Sari

headscarf

höfuðslæða

turban

túrban

burqa

búrka

kaftan

kaftan

abaya

abaya

swimsuit

sundföt

trunks

sundbuxur

shorts

stuttbuxur

tracksuit

íþróttagalli

apron

svunta

gloves

hanskar

button

hnappur

glasses

gleraugu

bracelet

armband

necklace

hálsmen

ring

hringur

earring

eyrnalokkur

cap

húfa

coat hanger

herðatré

hat

hattur

tie

bindi

zip

rennilás

helmet

hjálmur

braces

axlabönd

school uniform

skólabúningur

uniform

einkennisbúningur

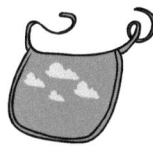

bib

smekkur

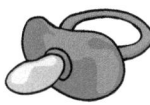

dummy

snuð

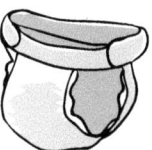

nappy

bleyja

office
skrifstofa

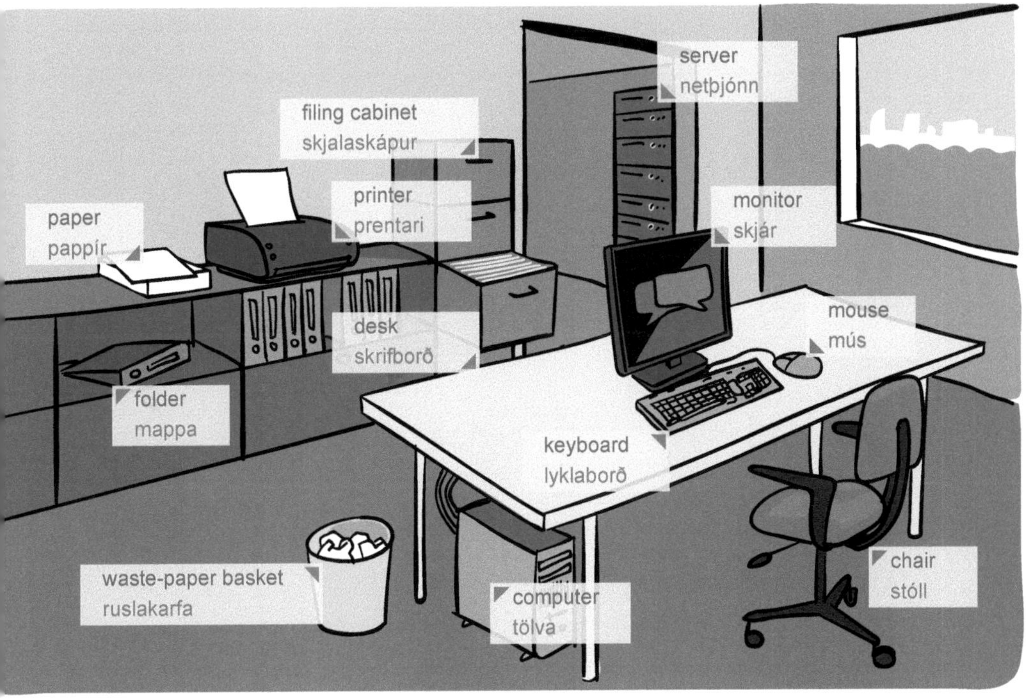

server
netþjónn
filing cabinet
skjalaskápur
printer
prentari
monitor
skjár
paper
pappír
desk
skrifborð
mouse
mús
folder
mappa
keyboard
lyklaborð
waste-paper basket
ruslakarfa
computer
tölva
chair
stóll

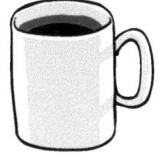

coffee mug

kaffibolli

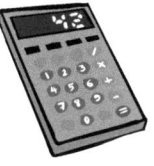

calculator

reiknivél

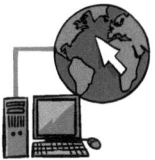

internet

internet

laptop

fartölva

letter

bréf

message

skilaboð

mobile

farsími

network

net

photocopier

ljósritunarvél

software

hugbúnaður

telephone

sími

plug socket

innstunga

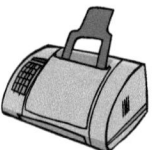

fax machine

faxtæki

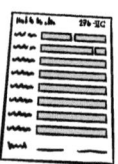

form

eyðublað

document

skjal

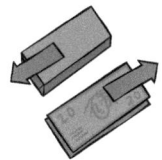

buy

kaupa

pay

borga

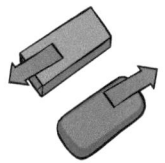

trade

versla

money

peningar

USD

dollar

dollari

EUR

euro

evra

JPY

yen

jen

RUB

rouble

rúbla

CHF

Swiss franc

svissneskur franki

CNY

renminbi yuan

renminbi yuan

INR

rupee

rúpíur

cashpoint

hraðbanki

bureau de change
gjaldeyrisskipti

gold
gull

silver
silfur

oil
olía

energy
orka

price
verð

contract
samningur

tax
skattur

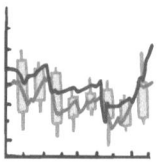

stock
hlutabréf

work
vinna

employee
starfsmaður

employer
vinnuveitandi

factory
verksmiðja

shop
búð

occupations
starfsgreinar

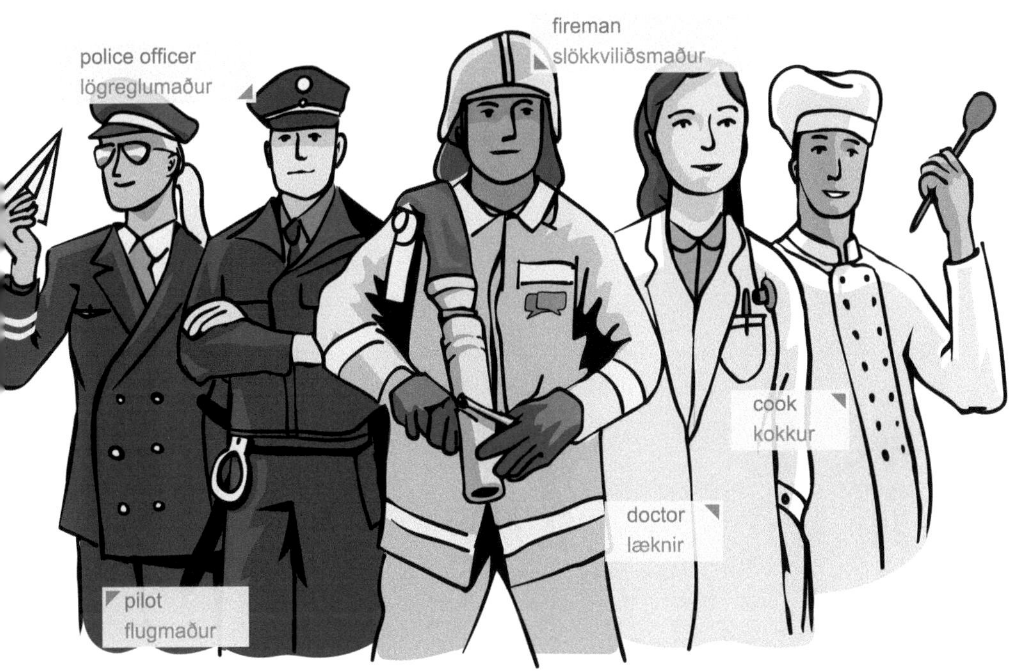
police officer
lögreglumaður
fireman
slökkviliðsmaður
cook
kokkur
doctor
læknir
pilot
flugmaður

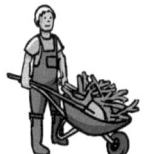

gardener

garðyrkjumaður

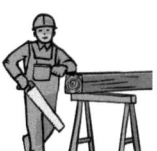

carpenter

smiður

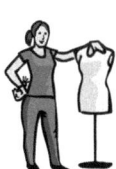

seamstress

saumakona

judge

dómari

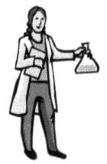

chemist

lyfjafræðingur

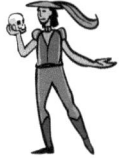

actor

leikari

bus driver

strætóbílstjóri

taxi driver

leigubílstjóri

fisherman

sjómaður

cleaning lady

ræstitæknir

roofer

þaksmiður

waiter

þjónn

hunter

veiðimaður

painter

málari

baker

bakari

electrician

rafvirki

builder

byggingaverkamaður

engineer

verkfræðingur

butcher

slátrari

plumber

pípari

postman

póstmaður

soldier
hermaður

architect
arkitekt

cashier
gjaldkeri

florist
blómasali

hairdresser
hárgreiðslumaður

conductor
lestarstjóri

mechanic
vélvirki

captain
skipstjóri

dentist
tannlæknir

scientist
vísindamaður

rabbi
rabbíi

imam
Imam

monk
munkur

clergyman
prestur

tools
verkfæri

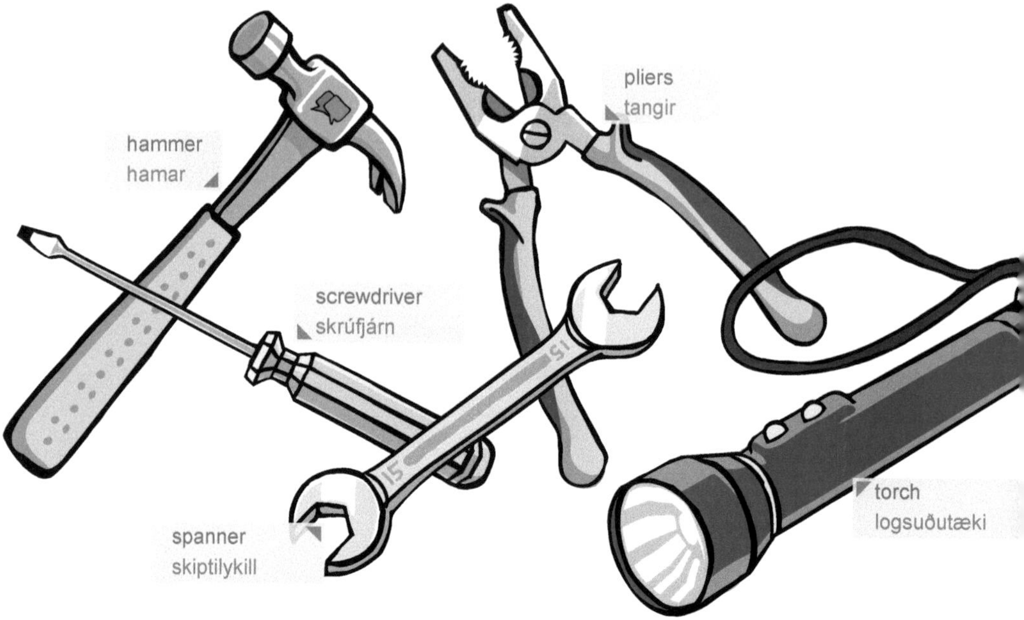

hammer
hamar
pliers
tangir
screwdriver
skrúfjárn
spanner
skiptilykill
torch
logsuðutæki

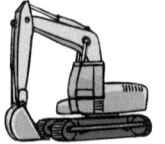

digger

grafa

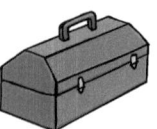

toolbox

verkfærataska

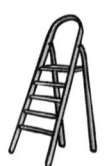

ladder

stigi

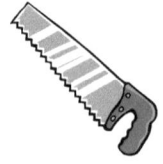

saw

sög

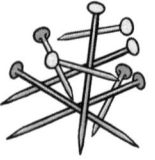

nails

naglar

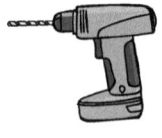

drill

bor

repair
gera við

shovel
skófla

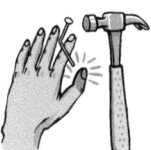

Damn!
Fjandinn!

dustpan
fægiskófla

paint pot
málningarfata

screws
skrúfur

musical instruments
hljóðfæri

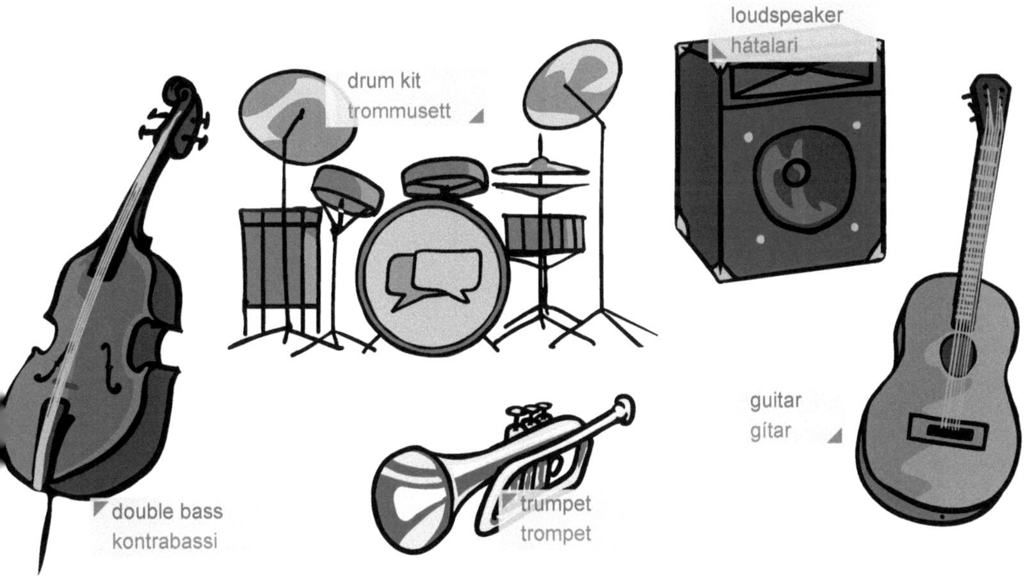

loudspeaker
hátalari

drum kit
trommusett

guitar
gítar

double bass
kontrabassi

trumpet
trompet

piano

píanó

violin

fiðla

bass

bassi

timpani

pákur

drums

trommur

keyboard

hljómborð

saxophone

saxófónn

flute

flauta

microphone

hljóðnemi

ZOO
dýragarður

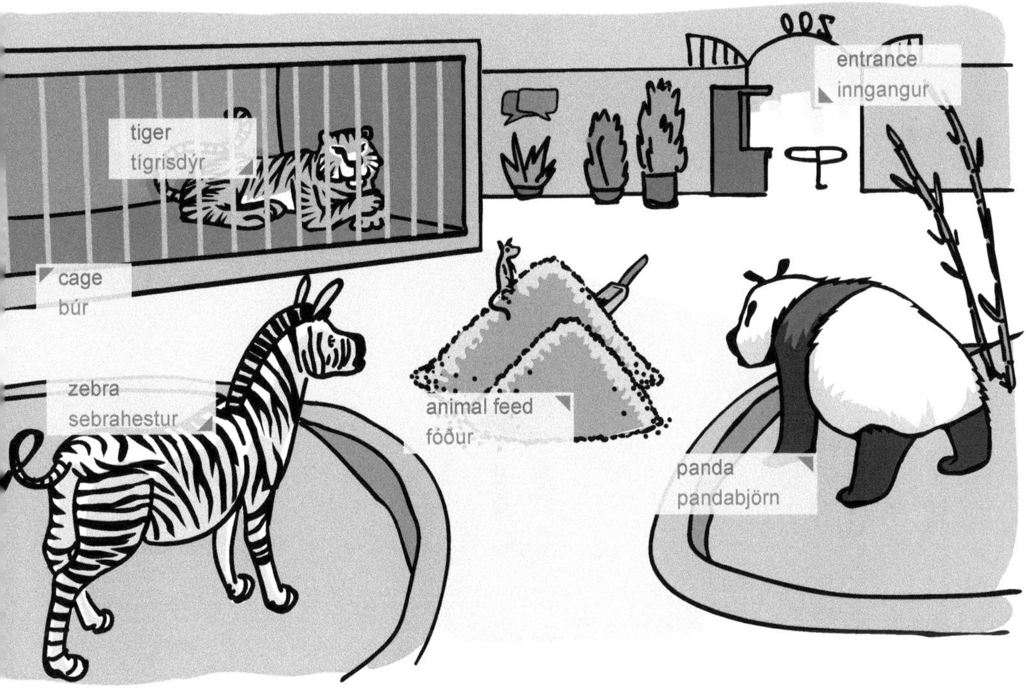
entrance
inngangur
tiger
tígrisdýr
cage
búr
zebra
sebrahestur
animal feed
fóður
panda
pandabjörn

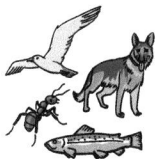

animals

dýr

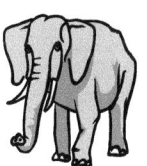

elephant

fíll

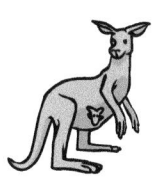

kangaroo

kengúra

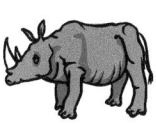

rhino

nashyrningur

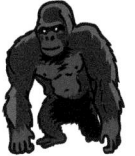

gorilla

górilla

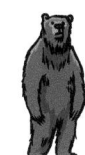

bear

skógarbjörn

camel

úlfaldi

ostrich

strútur

lion

ljón

monkey

api

flamingo

flamingó

parrot

páfagaukur

polar bear

ísbjörn

penguin

mörgæs

shark

hákarl

peacock

páfugl

snake

snákur

crocodile

krókódíll

zookeeper

dýragarðsvörður

seal

selur

jaguar

jagúar

pony

hestur

leopard

hlébarði

hippo

flóðhestur

giraffe

gíraffi

eagle

örn

boar

villisvín

fish

fiskur

turtle

skjaldbaka

walrus

rostungur

fox

refur

gazelle

gasella

American football
Amerískur fótbolti

cycling
hjólreiðar

tennis
tennis

basketball
körfubolti

swimming
sund

boxing
hnefaleikar

ice hockey
íshokkí

football
fótbolti

badminton
hnit

athletics
frjálsar íþróttir

handball
handbolti

skiing
skíði

polo
póló

jump
hoppa

laugh
hlæja

hug
faðma

walk
ganga

sing
syngja

dream
dreyma

pray
biðja

kiss
kyssa

write
skrifa

draw
teikna

show
sýna

push
ýta

give
gefa

take
taka

have
hafa

do
gera

be
vera

stand
standa

run
hlaupa

pull
draga

throw
kasta

fall
detta

lie
ljúga

wait
bíða

carry
bera

sit
sitja

get dressed
klæða sig

sleep
sofa

wake up
vakna

look at

líta á

cry

gráta

stroke

strjúka

comb

greiða

talk

tala

understand

skilja

ask

spyrja

listen

hlusta

drink

drekka

eat

borða

tidy up

taka til

love

elska

cook

elda

drive

keyra

fly

fljúga

sail

sigla

calculate

reikna

read

lesa

learn

læra

work

vinna

marry

giftast

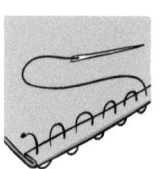

sew

sauma

brush teeth

bursta tennur

kill

drepa

smoke

reykja

send

senda

family
fjölskylda

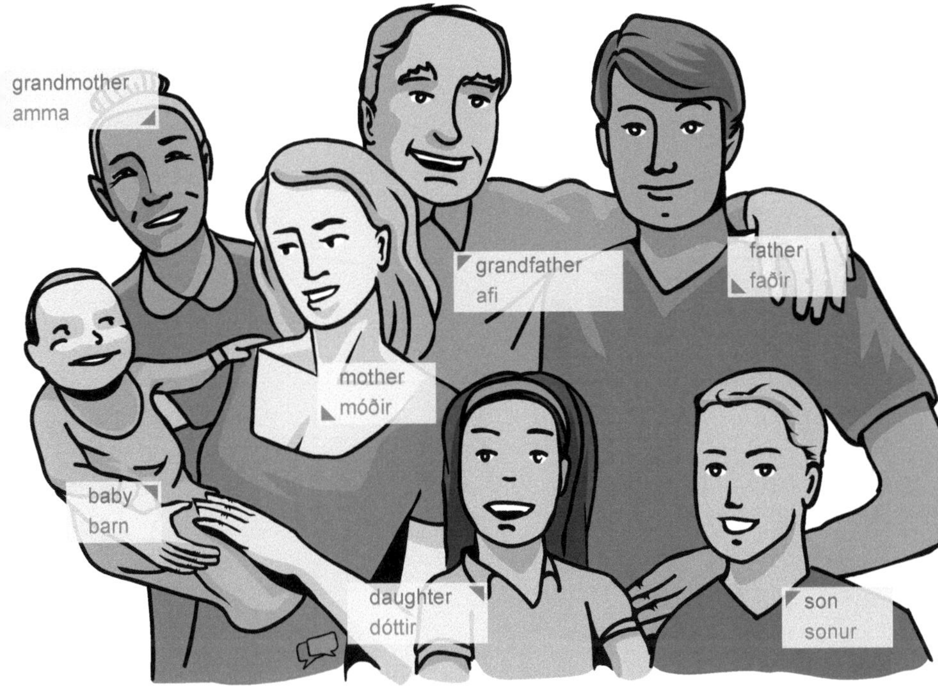
grandmother
amma
grandfather
afi
father
faðir
mother
móðir
baby
barn
daughter
dóttir
son
sonur

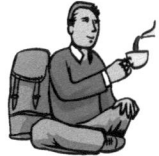

guest

gestur

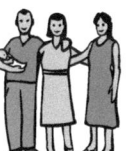

aunt

frænka

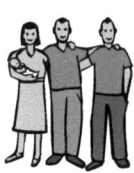

uncle

frændi

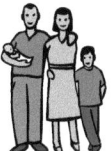

brother

bróðir

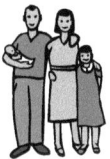

sister

systir

body
líkami

forehead
enni
eye
auga
shoulder
öxl
finger
fingur
face
andlit
chin
haka
hand
hönd
leg
fótleggur
breast
brjóst
arm
handleggur

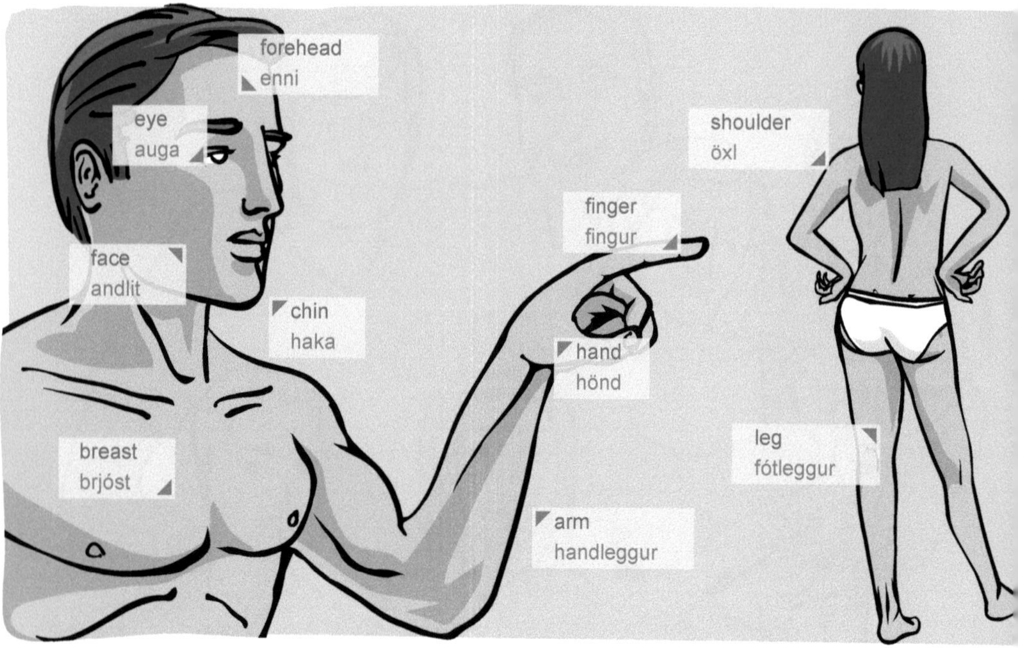

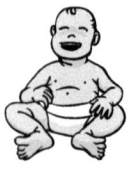

baby
barn

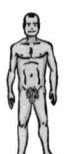

man
maður

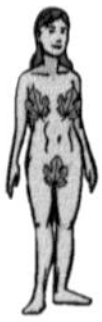

woman
kona

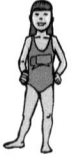

girl
stúlka

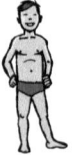

boy
drengur

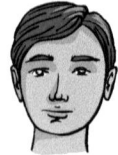

head
höfuð

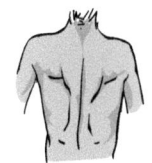

back

bak

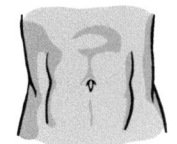

belly

kviður

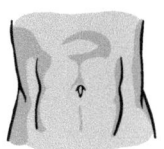

belly button

nafli

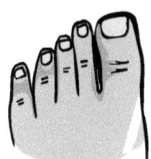

toe

tá

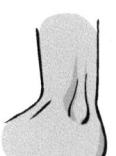

heel

hæll

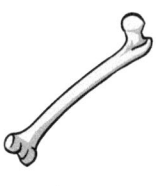

bone

bein

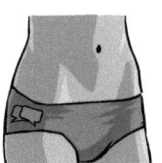

hip

mjöðm

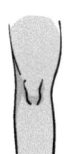

knee

hné

elbow

olnbogi

nose

nef

bottom

rass

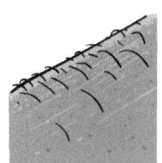

skin

húð

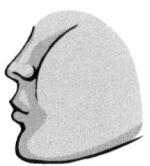

cheek

kinn

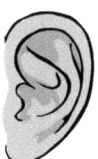

ear

eyra

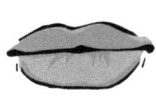

lip

vör

mouth
....
munnur

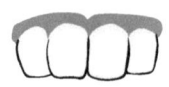

tooth
....
tönn

tongue
....
tunga

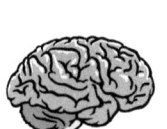

brain
....
heili

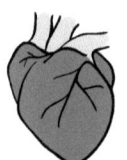

heart
....
hjarta

muscle
....
vöðvi

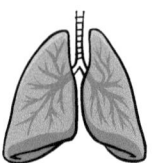

lung
....
lunga

liver
....
lifur

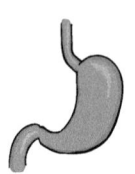

stomach
....
magi

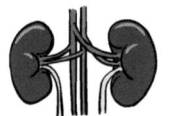

kidneys
....
nýru

sex
....
kynmök

condom
....
smokkur

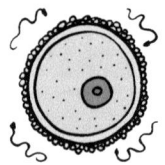

ovum
....
eggfruma

semen
....
sæði

pregnancy
....
ólétta

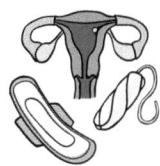

menstruation

tíðir

vagina

leggöng

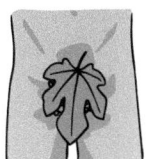

penis

typpi

eyebrow

augabrún

hair

hár

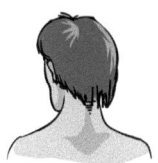

neck

háls

hospital
sjúkrahús

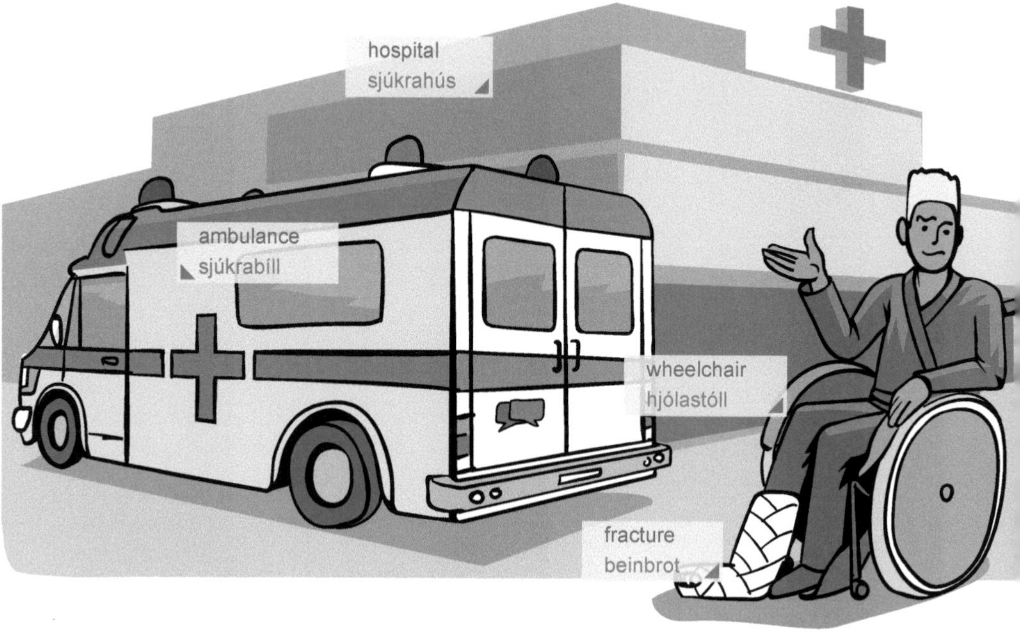

hospital
sjúkrahús
ambulance
sjúkrabíll
wheelchair
hjólastóll
fracture
beinbrot

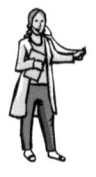

doctor
læknir

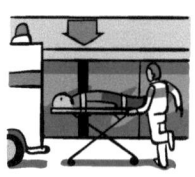

emergency room
bráðamóttaka

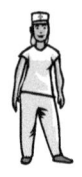

nurse
hjúkrunarfræðingur

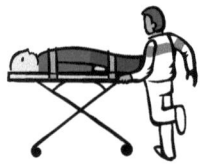

emergency
neyðartilvik

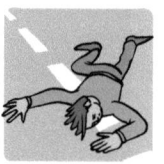

unconscious
meðvitundarlaus

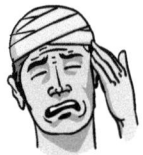

pain
verkir

injury

meiðsli

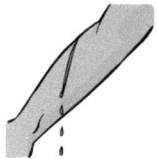

bleeding

blæðing

heart attack

hjartaáfall

stroke

heilablóðfall

allergy

ofnæmi

cough

hósti

fever

hiti

flu

flensa

diarrhoea

niðurgangur

headache

höfuðverkur

cancer

krabbamein

diabetes

sykursýki

surgeon

skurðlæknir

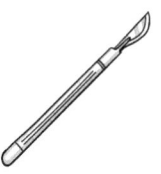

scalpel

skurðhnífur

operation

aðgerð

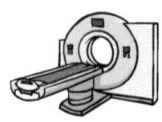

CT
sneiðmyndataka

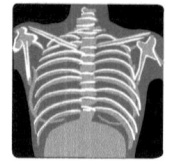

x-ray
röntgengeisli

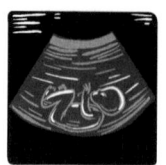

ultrasound
ómskoðun

face mask
andlitsgríma

disease
sjúkdómur

waiting room
biðstofa

crutch
hækja

plaster
gifs

bandage
sáraumbúðir

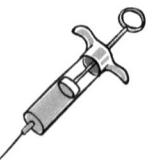

injection
sprauta

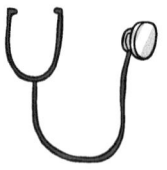

stethoscope
hlustunarpípa

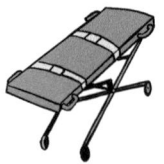

stretcher
börur

clinical thermometer
líkamshitamælir

birth
fæðing

overweight
yfirvigt

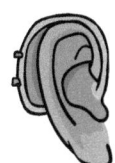

hearing aid
heyrnartæki

disinfectant
sótthreinsiefni

infection
sýking

virus
veira

HIV / AIDS
HIV / AIDS

medicine
lyf

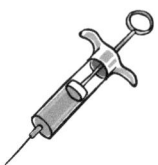

vaccination
bólusetning

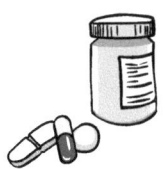

tablets
töflur

pill
pilla

emergency call
neyðarsímtal

blood pressure monitor
blóðþrýstingsmælir

ill / healthy
lasinn / heilbrigður

Help!

Hjálp!

alarm

viðvörun

assault

líkamsárás

attack

árás

danger

hætta

emergency exit

neyðarútgangur

Fire!

Eldur!

fire extinguisher

slökkvitæki

accident

slys

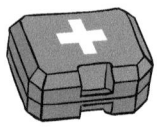

first-aid kit

skyndihjálparbúnaður

SOS

SOS

police

lögregla

Europe

Evrópa

North America

Norður-Ameríka

South America

Suður-Ameríka

Africa

Afríka

Asia

Asía

Australia

Ástralía

Atlantic

Atlantshaf

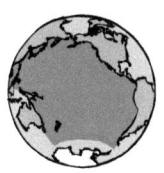

Pacific

Kyrrahaf

Indian Ocean

Indlandshaf

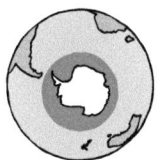

Antarctic Ocean

Suður-Íshaf

Arctic Ocean

Norður-Íshaf

North Pole

Norðurpóll

South Pole

Suðurpóll

Antarctica

Suðurskautslandið

Earth

Jörð

land

land

sea

sjór

island

eyja

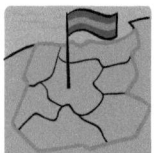

nation

þjóð

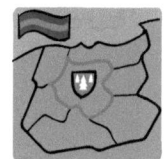

state

ríki

clock face

klukkuskífa

hour hand

litli vísir

minute hand

stóri vísir

second hand

sekúnduvísir

What time is it?

Hvað er klukkan?

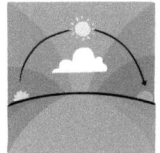

day

dagur

time

tími

now

nú

digital watch

tölvuúr

minute

mínúta

hour

klukkustund

week
vika

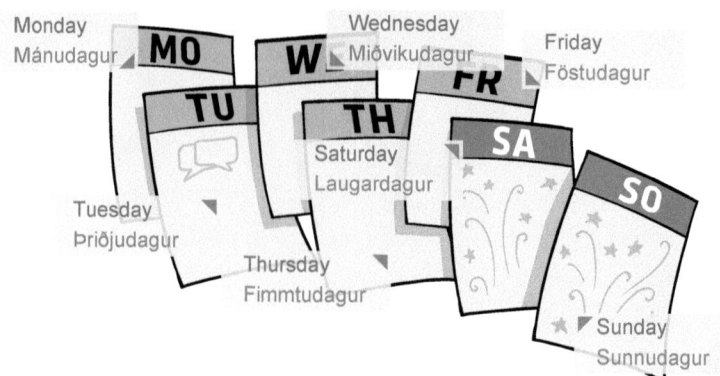

Monday
Mánudagur

Wednesday
Miðvikudagur

Friday
Föstudagur

Tuesday
Þriðjudagur

Thursday
Fimmtudagur

Saturday
Laugardagur

Sunday
Sunnudagur

yesterday

í gær

today

í dag

tomorrow

á morgun

morning

morgunn

noon

hádegi

evening

kvöld

business days

virkir dagar

weekend

helgi

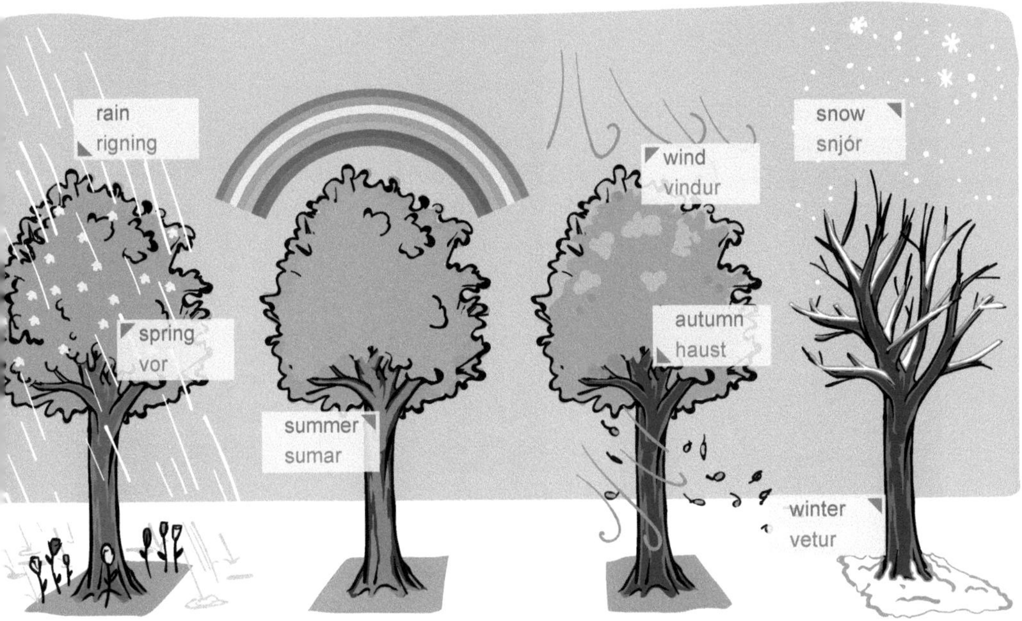

| rain | | wind | snow |
| rigning | | vindur | snjór |

spring
vor

summer
sumar

autumn
haust

winter
vetur

4.APRIL	11°	☀
5.APRIL	4°	🌧
6.APRIL	13°	🌬
7.APRIL	8°	❄
8.APRIL	10°	☀

weather forecast

veðurspá

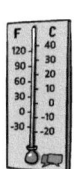

thermometer

hitamælir

sunshine

sólskin

cloud

ský

fog

þoka

humidity

raki

lightning

eldingar

thunder

þrumuveður

storm

stormur

hail

haglél

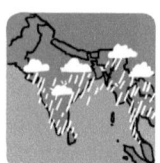

monsoon

monsún

flood

flóð

ice

ís

January

Janúar

February

Febrúar

March

Mars

April

Apríl

May

Maí

June

Júní

July

Júlí

August

Ágúst

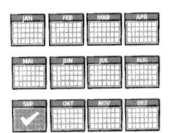

September
September

October
Október

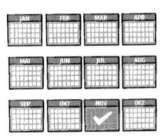

November
Nóvember

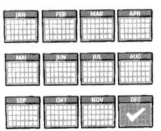

December
Desember

shapes
form

circle
hringur

square
ferningur

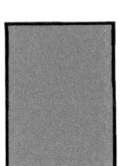

rectangle
rétthyrningur

triangle
þríhyrningur

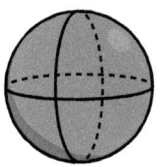

sphere
kúla

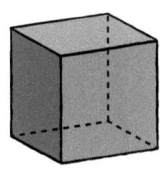

cube
teningur

white
hvítur

yellow
gulur

orange
appelsínugulur

pink
bleikur

red
rauður

purple
fjólublár

blue
blár

green
grænn

brown
brúnn

grey
grár

black
svartur

a lot / a little

mikið / lítið

angry / calm

reiður / rólegur

beautiful / ugly

fallegur / ljótur

beginning / end

upphaf / endir

big / small

stór / lítill

bright / dark

bjartur / dimmur

brother / sister

bróðir / systir

clean / dirty

hreinn / óhreinn

complete / incomplete

heill / ófullnægjandi

day / night

dagur / nótt

dead / alive

dauður / lifandi

wide / narrow

breiður / mjór

edible / inedible

ætur / óætur

evil / kind

vondur / góður

excited / bored

spenntur / leiður

fat / thin

feitur / mjór

first / last

fyrstur / síðastur

friend / enemy

vinur / óvinur

full / empty

fullur / tómur

hard / soft

harður / mjúkur

heavy / light

þungur / léttur

hunger / thirst

svangur / þyrstur

ill / healthy

lasinn / heilbrigður

illegal / legal

ólöglegur / löglegur

intelligent / stupid

greindur / heimskur

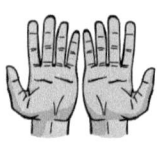

left / right

vinstri / hægri

near / far

nálægur / fjarlægur

new / used
nýr / notaður

nothing / something
ekkert / eitthvað

old / young
gamall / ungur

on / off
kveikt / slökkt

open / closed
opna / loka

quiet / loud
Lágvær / hávær

rich / poor
ríkur / fátækur

right / wrong
rétt / rangt

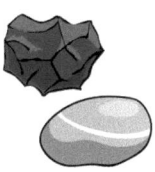

rough / smooth
grófur / sléttur

sad / happy
orgbitinn / hamingjusamur

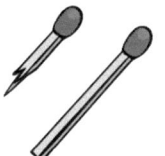

short / long
stutt / lengi

slow / fast
hægt / hratt

wet / dry
blautur / þurr

warm / cool
heitur / kaldur

war / peace
stríð / friður

0

zero

núll

1

one

einn

2

two

tveir

3

three

þrír

4

four

fjórir

5

five

fimm

6

six

sex

7

seven

sjö

8

eight

átta

9

nine

níu

10

ten

tíu

11

eleven

ellefu

12

twelve

tólf

13

thirteen

þrettán

14

fourteen

fjórtán

15

fifteen

fimmtán

16

sixteen

sextán

17

seventeen

sautján

18

eighteen

átján

19

nineteen

nítján

20

twenty

tuttugu

100

hundred

hundrað

1.000

thousand

þúsund

1.000.000

million

milljón

numbers - tölur

English

Enska

American English

Amerísk enska

Chinese Mandarin

Mandarin-kínverska

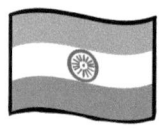

Hindi

Hindi

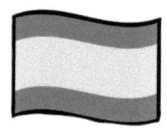

Spanish

Spænska

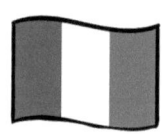

French

Franska

Arabic

Arabíska

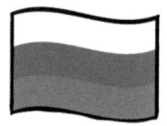

Russian

Rússneska

Portuguese

Portúgalska

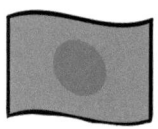

Bengali

Bengali

German

Þýska

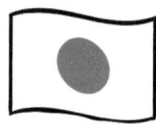

Japanese

Japanska

I
ég

you
þú

he / she / it
hann / hún / það

we
við

you
þú

they
þeir

who?
hver?

what?
hvað?

how?
hvernig?

where?
hvar?

when?
hvenær?

name
nafn

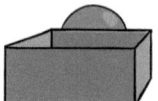

behind

bakvið

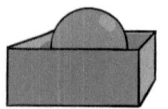

in

í

in front of

fyrir framan

over

yfir

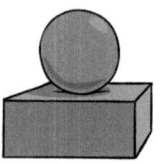

on

á

under

undir

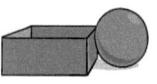

beside

við hliðina

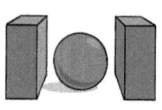

between

milli

place

sæti